ISLAM AND
BARACK HUSSEIN
OBAMA

ISLAM AND BARACK HUSSEIN OBAMA

A HANDBOOK ON ISLAM

Stephen M. Kirby Ph.D.

ISBN 1453682635

EAN-13 9781453682630

*Over the last fifteen months, we've traveled to every
corner of the United States. I've now been in 57 states, I
think — one left to go...*

Senator Barack Hussein Obama, Democratic Presidential Candidate, May
9, 2008, Beaverton, Oregon

Reality: There are only 50 states in the United States. However,
there are 57 states who are members of the Organization of the
Islamic Conference (OIC). The OIC, established in 1969, "is the
collective voice of the Muslim world and ensuring to safeguard
and protect the interests of the Muslim world..." http://www.oic-
oci.org/page_detail.asp?p_id=52

*...we have to educate ourselves more effectively on Islam.
And one of the points I want to make is, is if you actually
took the number of Muslims [sic] Americans, we'd be one
of the largest Muslim countries in the world.*

President Barack Hussein Obama, in an interview on June 1, 2009 with
French Correspondent Laura Haim, of Canal Plus

Reality: According to the October 2009 Pew Research
Center report *Mapping the Global Muslim Population*, there
are 54 countries in the world with larger Muslim populations
than the United States .

http://www.pewforum.org/Muslim/Mapping-the-Global-
Muslim-Population.aspx

We know too that whatever our differences, there is one law that binds all great religions together. Jesus told us to "love thy neighbor as thyself." The Torah commands, "That which is hateful to you, do not do to your fellow." In Islam, there is a hadith that reads "None of you truly believes until he wishes for his brother what he wishes for himself."

President Barack Hussein Obama, February 5, 2009, White House National Prayer Breakfast

---

Reality:

Muhammad said: *None of you will have faith till he wishes for his (Muslim)* [sic] *brother what he likes for himself.*

Hadith - al-Bukhari, Volume1, Book 2, Number 12

Chapter 18: Concerning the fact that it is one of the characteristics of Iman [Faith] that one should like the same thing for one's brother-in-Islam as one likes for one's self

Hadith – Muslim, Book 1: The Book of Faith (Kitab Al-Iman)

Understanding the role of the Muslim Brother in North America:

The process of settlement is a "Civilization-Jihadist Process" with all the word means. The Ikhwan [Muslim Brotherhood] *must understand that their work in America is a kind of grand Jihad in eliminating and destroying the Western civilization from within and "sabotaging" its miserable house by their hands and the hands of the believers* [Muslims] *so that it is eliminated and God's religion* [Islam] *is made victorious over all other religions. Without this level of understanding, we are not up to this challenge and have not prepared ourselves for Jihad yet. It is a Muslim's destiny to perform Jihad and work wherever he is and wherever he lands until the final hour comes, and there is no escape from that destiny except for those who chose to slack...*

An Explanatory Memorandum on the General Strategic Goal for the Group in North America, May 22, 1991

Bate #ISE-SW 1B10/0000418 - From a copy of the Memorandum introduced as evidence in the federal trial against the Holy Land Foundation for Relief and Development.

In 2001, the Foundation, one of the largest Islamic charitable organizations in the United States, was accused of providing support to Hamas, a designated foreign terrorist organization. The Foundation was shut down by the United States Treasury Department in December of 2001.

On November 24, 2008, the Foundation and five of its leaders were convicted on charges of providing material support to Hamas. The five leaders subsequently received sentences ranging from 15 to 65 years in federal prison.

Stoning to Death

The legal penalty is obligatorily imposed upon anyone who fornicates or commits sodomy...If the offender is someone with the capacity to remain chaste, then he or she is stoned to death...If the penalty is stoning, the offender is stoned even in severe heat or cold, and even if he has an illness from which he is expected to recover. A pregnant woman is not stoned until she gives birth and the child can suffice with the milk of another.

Reliance of the Traveller (Umdat al-Salik), A Classic Manual of Islamic Sacred Law, o12.0

Muhammad ordered it:

The apostle said: I am the first to revive the order of God and His book and to practice it [stoning].

Muhammad Ibn Ishaq, *The Life of Muhammad (Sirat Rasul Allah)*, p. 267.

Hadith - al-Bukhari, Volume 6, Book 60, Number 79:

Narrated 'Abdullah bin Umar: The Jews brought to the Prophet [Muhammad] a man and a woman from among them who had committed illegal sexual intercourse. The Prophet said to them, "How do you usually punish the one amongst you who has committed illegal sexual intercourse?" They replied, "We blacken their faces with coal and beat them," He said, "Don't you find the order of Ar-Rajm (i.e. stoning to death) in the Torah?" They replied, "We do not find anything in it." 'Abdullah bin Salam (after hearing this conversation) said to them. "You have told a lie! Bring here the Torah and recite it if you are truthful." (So the Jews brought the Torah). And the religious teacher who was teaching it to them, put his hand over the Verse of Ar-Rajm and started reading what was written above and below the place hidden with his hand, but he did not read the Verse of Ar-Rajm. 'Abdullah bin Salam removed his (i.e. the teacher's) hand from the Verse of Ar-Rajm and said, "What is this?" So when the Jews saw that Verse, they said, "This is the Verse of Ar-Rajm." So the Prophet ordered the two adulterers to be stoned to death, and they were stoned to death near the place where biers used to be placed near the Mosque. I saw her companion (i.e. the adulterer) bowing over her so as to protect her from the stones.

Hadith - Muslim, Book 017, Number 4206:

'Abdullah b. Buraida reported on the authority of his father that....There came to him (the Holy Prophet [Muhammad]) a woman from Ghamid and said: Allah's Messenger, I have committed adultery, so purify me. He (the Holy Prophet) turned her away. On the following day she said: Allah's Messenger, Why do you turn me away?...By Allah, I have become pregnant. He said: Well, if you insist upon it, then go away until you give birth to (the child). When she was delivered she came with the child (wrapped) in a rag and said: Here is the child whom I have given birth to. He said: Go away and suckle him until you wean him. When she had weaned him, she came to him (the Holy Prophet) with the child who was holding a piece of bread in his hand. She said: Allah's Apostle, here is he as I have weaned him and he eats food. He (the Holy Prophet) entrusted the child to one of the Muslims and then pronounced punishment. And she was put in a ditch up to her chest and he commanded people and they stoned her.

Table of Contents

Introduction

How do you reconcile the peaceful verses with the violent verses in the Koran? Is violent extremism irreconcilable with Islam? How well are women treated under Islam? Would it be an example of *taqiyya* if a Muslim denied the accuracy of *Sahih* Hadiths or of the information found in the *Sira*? When you have finished reading this handbook, you will have answers to these questions and others, and you will have more knowledge about Islam than do most Americans. You will also know where in Islamic sources to direct those who might be skeptical about what you have learned.

There are two sections to this handbook. The second, smaller section looks at the shooting of two United States Army privates by a Muslim convert on June 1, 2009 in Little Rock, Arkansas. The ensuing two day silence and then the nature of the subsequent response from President Barack Hussein Obama, their Commander-in-Chief, are cause for questions and concern, especially when contrasted with how Obama responded to other deaths during that time period. And why would the natural death of an allegedly corrupt ruler of a small African nation receive more presidential attention than the murder and severe wounding of United States military personnel, on American soil, by a Muslim convert?

The majority of this handbook is dedicated to comparing the reality of Islam with many of the claims about Islam made by President Obama in his June 4, 2009 speech in Cairo, Egypt. The contrast is startling, especially when Obama had proclaimed early in his speech

> ...*partnership between America and Islam **must be based on what Islam is, not what it isn't.*** [my emphasis]

In order to understand the magnitude of that contrast, it is important to have a basic understanding of Islam. To learn about and gain an understanding of Islam, one must not only consider the Koran, the sacred book of Islam, but also the *Sunna* (the Way of Muhammad, the founder of Islam, who is also referred to, inter alia, as Allah's prophet, messenger, or apostle). The *Sunna* is based mainly on the hadiths (*ahadith*), which are reports about the examples and teachings of Muhammad believed to have come from those who knew him. The most reliable collection of hadiths is that compiled by an Islamic scholar named al-Bukhari; the second most reliable is that compiled by an Islamic scholar named Muslim. These two hadith collections are referred to as *sahih* (sound, authentic). The *Sunna* is also based on another source of accepted knowledge, the *Sira*, the authoritative biography of Muhammad written in the eighth century by Muhammad Ibn Ishaq. Finally, one must also take into consideration Sharia Law (Islamic Sacred Law), which can be found in a reference book titled *Reliance of the Traveller (Umdat al Salik), A Classic Manual of Islamic Sacred Law*. I consulted these sources in examining the claims about Islam made by President Obama.

One commonly heard response when talking about verses in the Koran is that the Koran cannot be accurately translated from the Arabic and one must therefore know that language in order to truly understand what is written. In the first place, there is a long history of writings being translated into other languages, so there would be nothing unique or insurmountable about translating the Koran from Arabic into another language; the main issue would be the accuracy of that translation (with unique consequences for a lack of such accuracy). Secondly, translations of the Koran have already been done by Muslims in an attempt to spread Islam to those who do not speak Arabic. An example of this is the English translation of the Koran provided to interested parties at no charge by the Council on American-Islamic Relations (CAIR).[1] In its 2006 Annual

---

[1]   *The Message of the Qur'an*, trans. Muhammad Asad, (Bristol, England: The Book Foundation, 2003). Here is CAIR's website statement about this

Report, CAIR noted that more than 30,000 people had received free copies of this Koran, and those people had "benefited from **the opportunity to read the holy text** [my emphasis]."[2] CAIR apparently did not have any concern about the accuracy of the translation of the Koran it was providing. And it is interesting to note that Muhammad Asad, the translator of this Koran, was actually an East European of Jewish origin who started learning Arabic in his early twenties and then soon converted to Islam.[3]

The translation of the Koran that I use in this handbook was done by Marmaduke Pickthall, an Englishman who had converted to Islam prior to writing that translation. As I point out in more detail in Footnote 19 of the section dealing with President Obama's Cairo speech, Pickthall had every incentive to make sure his translation was accurate because it was and is apostasy for a Muslim to revile Allah or Muhammad, or to deny any verse of the Koran or to add a verse that does not belong to it. This is a law that is still very much in effect. For example, in February 2009, two Afghans, who originally faced the death sentence, were each sentenced to 20 years in prison for making mistakes in translating the Koran.[4]

---

translation (http://www.explorethequran.com/about-the-quran/about-this-quran.html):

> *The Muhammad Asad translation offered through CAIR's Share the Quran campaign is produced by the Book Foundation. This magnificent production contains the Arabic text, the English translation, the English transliteration and footnotes.*

[2]   *Results that Speak for Themselves, CAIR 2006 Annual Report*, p. 9, accessible at: http://www.cair.com/Portals/0/pdf/2006_Annual_Report.pdf.

[3]   Asad was born Leopold Weiss, "the grandson of an Orthodox Rabbi," in 1900 in Lwow (Lvov), in what is now Poland. He converted to Islam in 1926 and died in Spain at the age of 92. See *The Message of the Qur'an*, pp. iv-v.

[4]   "Jail upheld in Afghan Koran case," BBC News, February 16, 2009, accessible at http://news.bbc.co.uk/2/hi/7893171.stm. For a more complete account of the event showing the influence of "hardline clerics," see "2 Afghans face death over translation of Quran," MSNBC World News, February 6, 2009, accessible at http://www.msnbc.msn.com/id/29049101/.

iii

The concept of "abrogation" is also important to understanding Islam. For this concept, we need to get a basic understanding of the Koran. The Koran is the sacred book of Islam, and it is considered by Muslims to be the infallible word of Allah "revealed" to the prophet Muhammad over 23 years. Muhammad was born in Mecca around 570 AD, and he began receiving the "revelations" around 610 AD while he was still in Mecca. He continued to receive them after he left Mecca and emigrated with some of his followers to Medina in 622 AD.[5] The 114 chapters (*suras*) of the Koran, however, are not arranged in chronological order, but rather arranged generally by the length of the chapter, starting with the longest chapter and then ending with the shortest chapter. Each chapter indicates whether it was "revealed" in Mecca or in Medina. In the Koran you will also find that the chapters of the earlier "revelations" from Mecca are interspersed among chapters of the later "revelations" from Medina.

While in Mecca, Muhammad was just starting the religion of Islam, and it was not generally well received. Perhaps as a result of this resistance, the Koranic verses "revealed" in Mecca were generally more peaceful and accommodating toward non-Muslims than the verses later "revealed" in Medina. The verses from Medina have a general tendency to be more belligerent and more inclined to make sharp differentiations between Muslims (believers) and non-Muslims (disbelievers). This can lead to a conflict between the message of a Meccan verse and that of a Medinan verse addressing the same general topic. But how can there be such a conflict if the Koran is the infallible, "revealed" word of Allah? This was covered in a Medinan verse that introduced the concept of "abrogation":

> *Such of Our revelations as We abrogate or cause to be forgotten, we bring (in place) one better or the like thereof. Knowest thou not that Allah is Able to do all things?* – Chapter 2, Verse 106[6]

---

[5] This emigration from Mecca to Medina is known as the *Hijrah* and marks the beginning point of the Islamic calendar.

[6] *The Meaning of The Glorious Koran*, trans. Marmaduke Pickthall, (1930; rpt. New York: Alfred A. Knopf, 1992). Subsequent verses quoted from the Koran are from this translation.

Abrogation means that if there is a conflict between the messages of two "revelations" in the Koran, then the most recent "revelation" is the one to be followed. Consequently, a "revelation" made in Medina would supersede a similar, earlier "revelation" made in Mecca if there was a conflict between the two.

For example, consider the Medinan "Verse of the Sword," Chapter 9, Verse 5:

> *Then, when the sacred months have passed, slay the*
> *idolaters wherever ye find them, and take them (captive),*
> *and besiege them, and prepare for them each ambush.*
> *But if they repent and establish worship and pay the poor-*
> *due, then leave their way free. Lo! Allah is Forgiving,*
> *Merciful.*

Robert Spencer noted that most Muslim authorities agree that Chapter 9 was the very last chapter of the Koran (Qur'an) to be "revealed," and some Islamic theologians maintained that Verse 5 had abrogated no fewer than 124 more peaceful and tolerant verses of the Koran; in fact, one Koran commentator believed that Verse 5 had abrogated "every peace treaty" in the Koran.[7]

David Bukay pointed out that Suyuti, an Egyptian theologian (d. 1505), said that everything in the Koran about forgiveness and peace was abrogated by the Verse of the Sword.[8] And Ibn Abbas, a cousin of the prophet Muhammad, had even stated that the Verse of the Sword abrogated a verse instructing Muslims to grant peace if infidels asked for peace.[9]

---

[7]   Robert Spencer, *The Politically Incorrect Guide to Islam (And The Crusades)*, (Washington DC: Regnery Publishing, Inc., 2005), p. 25.

[8]   David Bukay, "Peace or Jihad? Abrogation in Islam," *The Middle East Quarterly*, Volume 14, No. 4 (Fall 2007). Accessible at http://www.meforum.org/1754/peace-or-jihad-abrogation-in-islam.

[9]   Robert Spencer, *The Complete Infidel's Guide to the Koran*, (Washington DC: Regnery Publishing, Inc., 2009), p. 217. That verse is Chapter

Spencer summed up the consequences of such abrogations:

> *All this means that warfare against unbelievers until they*
> *either become Muslim or pay the jizya – the special tax on*
> *non-Muslims in Islamic law – "with willing submission"*
> *(Qur'an 9:29) is the Qur'an's last word on jihad.*
> *Mainstream Islamic tradition has interpreted this as*
> *Allah's enduring marching orders to the human race: The*
> *Islamic umma (community) must exist in a state of*
> *perpetual war with the non-Muslim world, punctuated*
> *only by temporary truces.*[10]

This is a point reiterated by David Bukay in considering the writings of a
contemporary Islamic scholar:

> *Muhammad Sa'id Ramadan al-Buti, a contemporary Al-*
> *Azhar University scholar, wrote that "the verse (9:5) does*
> *not leave any room in the mind to conjecture about what*
> *is called defensive war. This verse asserts that holy war,*
> *which is demanded in Islamic law, is not a defensive war*
> *because it could legitimately be an offensive war. That is*
> *the apex and most honorable of all holy wars. Its goal is*
> *the exaltation of the word of God, the construction of*
> *Islamic society, and the establishment of God's kingdom*
> *on earth regardless of the means. It is legal to carry on an*
> *offensive holy war."*[11]

8, Verse 61: *And if they incline to peace, incline thou also to it, and trust in Allah.*
Lo! He is the Hearer, the Knower.

[10] Spencer, *The Politically Incorrect Guide to Islam*, p. 26. Here is Chapter
9, Verse 29 of the Koran:

> *Fight against such of those who have been given the*
> *Scripture as believe not in Allah nor the Last Day, and*
> *forbid not that which Allah hath forbidden by His*
> *messenger, and follow not the religion of truth, until*
> *they pay the tribute readily, being brought low.*

[11] Bukay.

And even the terrorist group Al-Qaeda found the Verse of the Sword, along with other Koranic verses, useful. In 1998, Al-Qaeda's declaration of war against the United States began by praising Allah for providing the Verse of the Sword.[12] This declaration of war also pointed out that

> *The ruling to kill the Americans and their allies – civilians and military – is an individual obligation incumbent upon every Muslim who can do it and in any country...This is in accordance with the Word of the Most High – [F]ight the pagans all together as they fight you all together" [9:36] and the Word of the Most High, "Fight them until there is no more tumult or oppression, and [all] religion belongs to Allah" [8.39].*[13]

So when being told about Koranic verses emphasizing accommodation and social harmony among religions, keep in mind the concept of abrogation and ask where and when the verses were revealed, and could they have been abrogated by the Verse of the Sword or similar Koranic verses?

It should be noted that the Koranic verses used in this handbook are Medinan.

There is another Islamic concept that is important to understand: *taqiyya*, which means deception directed at non-Muslims. In talking about *taqiyya*, Robert Spencer said:

> *It's unfortunate, but true: Islam is the only major religion with a developed doctrine of deception.*[14]

---

[12]   *The Al Qaeda Reader*, edited and translated by Raymond Ibrahim, (New York: Broadway Books, 2007), page 11.

[13]   Ibid., p. 13. The Koranic chapter and verse numbers in brackets were provided by Ibrahim. It is interesting to note how heavily Al Qaeda relies on Koranic verses to justify its hostility and war against the West.

[14]   Spencer, *The Complete Infidel's Guide to the Koran*, p. 202.

In terms of Sharia Law, there appears to be a legal basis for this doctrine. In a section titled "Permissible Lying," Imam Abu Hamid Ghazali, a noted early Islamic scholar wrote:

> *If a praiseworthy aim is attainable through both telling the truth and lying, it is unlawful to accomplish through lying **because there is no need for it*** [my emphasis]. *When it is possible to achieve such an aim by lying but not by telling the truth, it is permissible to lie if attaining the goal is permissible, and obligatory to lie if the goal is obligatory....Whether the purpose is war, settling a disagreement, or gaining the sympathy of a victim legally entitled to retaliate against one so that he will forbear to do so; it is not unlawful to lie when any of these aims can only be attained through lying.*[15]

And there also appears to be a doctrinal basis for *taqiyya*. Raymond Ibrahim pointed out that the following Koranic verse "is often seen as the primary verse that sanctions deception towards non-Muslims":[16]

> Chapter 3, Verse 28: *Let not the believers take disbelievers for their friends in preference to believers. Whoso doeth that hath no connection with Allah unless (it be) that ye but guard yourselves against them, taking (as it were) security. Allah biddeth you beware (only) of Himself. Unto Allah is the journeying.*

Ibrahim wrote that Tabari, the author of "a standard and authoritative" Koran commentary had explained this verse in this manner:

---

[15]   *Reliance of the Traveller (Umdat al-Salik), A Classic Manual of Islamic Sacred Law*, Ahmad ibn Naqib al-Misri, edited and translated by Nuh Ha Mim Keller, (Beltsville, Maryland: Amana Publications, Revised edition, 2008), r8.2.

[16]   Raymond Ibrahim, "How Taqiyya Alters Islam's Rules of War, Defeating Jihadist Terrorism," *The Middle East Quarterly*, Volume 17, No. 1 (Winter 2010). Accessible at http://www.meforum.org/2538/taqiyya-islam-rules-of-war.

*If you [Muslims] are under their [non-Muslims']
authority, fearing for yourselves, behave loyally to them
with your tongue while harboring inner animosity for
them...[know that] God has forbidden believers from
being friendly or on intimate terms with the infidels rather
than other believers – expect when infidels are above them
[in authority]. Should that be the case, let them act
friendly towards them while preserving their religion.*[17]

And *taqiyya* appears to be a concept widely known and practiced in Islam.
As Ibrahim noted, a contemporary Islamic scholar had written that

*Taqiyya is of fundamental importance in Islam.
Practically every Islamic sect agrees to it and practices
it...We can go so far as to say that the practice of taqiyya
is mainstream in Islam, and that those few sects not
practicing it diverge from the mainstream...Taqiyya is
very prevalent in Islamic politics, especially in the modern
era.*[18]

There is no intent here to claim that every Muslim believes in *taqiyya*
and/or acts in a deceitful manner toward non-Muslims. But Ibrahim makes
a disquieting observation about the implications of *taqiyya*:

*Islamic law unambiguously splits the world into two
perpetually warring halves—the Islamic world versus the
non-Islamic—and holds it to be God's will for the former
to subsume the latter. Yet if war with the infidel is a
perpetual affair, if war is deceit, and if deeds are justified
by intentions—any number of Muslims will naturally
conclude that they have a divinely sanctioned right to
deceive, so long as they believe their deception serves to
aid Islam "until all chaos ceases, and all religion belongs
to God." Such deception will further be seen as a means
to an altruistic end. Muslim overtures for peace, dialogue,*

---

[17]   Ibid.

[18]   Ibid.

ix

or even temporary truces must be seen in this light, evoking the practical observations of philosopher James Lorimer, uttered over a century ago: "So long as Islam endures, the reconciliation of its adherents, even with Jews and Christians, and still more with the rest of mankind, must continue to be an insoluble problem."[19]

Stephen M. Kirby

---

[19]   Ibid. Islamic Sacred Law divides the world into only two categories: dar al-Islam (House of Islam/Muslim Lands) and dar al-Harb (House of War/Enemy Lands) – see *Reliance of the Traveller*, w43.5.

President Obama's Speech to the Muslim World

Introduction

On June 4, 2009, President Barack Hussein Obama gave a speech to the Muslim world from Cairo University in Cairo, Egypt.[1] He presented it from the unique perspective of having lived in Indonesia and having gone to a "Muslim school" for two years as a youth.[2] In a March 2007 interview with *New York Times* columnist Nicholas Kristof, Obama had described himself as "a little Jakarta street kid," who got into trouble for making faces during his Koran study classes; Kristof noted that during the interview Obama "recalled the opening lines of the Arabic [sic] call to

---

[1] For the text of the speech, go to the White House website: www.whitehouse.gov/the_press_office/Remarks-by-the-President-at-Cairo-University-6-04-09

[2] Obama was six years old when he moved with his family to Indonesia in 1967. In 1971 his mother sent him to Hawaii to live with his grandparents. During his teenage years he returned to Indonesia for three or four short visits. See Barack Obama, *The Audacity of Hope*, (New York: Crown Publishers, 2006), pp. 273-276. For his attendance at a "Muslim school" for two years, see Barack Obama, *Dreams from My Father*, (New York: Crown Publishers, 2004), p. 154.

prayer, reciting them with a first-rate accent," and Obama had described this call to prayer as "one of the prettiest sounds on Earth at sunset."[3] This call to prayer includes the declaration that Allah is greatest and the testimony that there is no god but Allah and Muhammad is the messenger of Allah; according to Obama then, this declaration and testimony made up "one of the prettiest sounds on Earth at sunset."[4]

---

[3]   Nicholas D. Kristof, "Obama: Man of the World," *New York Times*, March 6, 2007. Accessible at http://select.nytimes.com/2007/03/06/opinion/06kristof.html?_r=1.

[4]   The words of the Call to Prayer (*Adhan*):

> *Allah is greatest [Allahu Akbar]. Allah is greatest. Allah is greatest. Allah is greatest. I testify there is no god [sic] but Allah. I testify there is no god but Allah. I testify that Muhammad is the Messenger of Allah. I testify that Muhammad is the Messenger of Allah. Come to the prayer. Come to the prayer. Come to success. Come to success. Allah is greatest. Allah is greatest. There is no god but Allah.*

Reliance of the Traveller (Umdat al-Salik), A Classic Manual of Islamic Sacred Law, Ahmad ibn Naqib al-Misri, edited and translated by Nuh Ha Mim Keller, (Beltsville, Maryland: Amana Publications, Revised edition, 2008), f3.6. In 1990, Dr. Taha Jabir al-Alwani, President of the Fiqh [Islamic Jurisprudence] Council of North America, and President of the International Institute of Islamic Thought located in Northern Virginia, said of this English translation (p. xviii):

> *There is no doubt that this translation is a valuable and important work, whether as a textbook for teaching Islamic jurisprudence to English-speakers, or as a legal reference for use by scholars, educated laymen, and students in this language...its aim is to imbue the consciousness of the non-Arabic-speaking Muslim with a sound understanding of Sacred Law...*

In 1991 this English translation was certified to correspond "to the Arabic original" and conform "to the practice and faith of the orthodox Sunni Community" by the Islamic Research Academy of Al-Azhar University in Cairo (p. xx). "Al-Azhar is considered by most Sunni Muslims to be the most prestigious school of Islamic law, and its scholars are seen as the highest scholars in the Muslim world." The Islamic Research Academy is considered to be the highest authority at Al-Azhar. See

2

Having attended Koran study classes and, as he said in this Cairo speech, being "a student of history" and having "known Islam on three continents," Obama seemed well prepared for his presentation.

Standing in front of the large audience at Cairo University that day, President Obama said

> *I've come here to Cairo to seek a new beginning between the United States and Muslims around the world...one based upon the truth that America and Islam are not exclusive and need not be in competition. Instead, they overlap, and share common principles -- principles of justice and progress; tolerance and the dignity of all human beings...There must be a sustained effort to listen to each other; to learn from each other; to respect one another; and to seek common ground. As the Holy Koran tells us, "Be conscious of God and speak always the truth." (Applause.) That is what I will try to do today -- to speak the truth as best I can...*

According to President Obama, the United States and the Muslim world were "not exclusive," but rather "overlap and share common principles." Over the following pages I will compare selected sections of Obama's speech with the reality of Islam based primarily on Islamic sources. This will allow the reader to decide how well President Obama spoke "the truth" about Islam.

Muslim Apostasy and the Establishment Clause

Obama told his audience, "I'm a Christian, but my father came from a Kenyan family that includes generations of Muslims," thereby allowing the implication that although there were Muslim relatives in Kenya, his father was not touched by Islam. However, in his book *The Audacity of Hope*, Obama had written

---

http://www.usislam.org/mosques/al_azhar_mosque.htm and
http://www.aawsat.com/english/news.asp?section=3&id=15494, respectively.

*...although my father had been raised a Muslim, by the
time he met my mother he was a confirmed atheist...*[5]

Obama could have repeated this explanation to his Muslim audience, but
he chose not to. I believe it is because he most likely knew that such an
explanation would have identified his father as an apostate from Islam, and
under Sharia Law (Islamic Sacred Law), such apostasy is punishable by
death.[6]

He also possibly knew that his audience could therefore consider him an
apostate from Islam as well. According to the teachings of Muhammad,
all children are born as Muslims (their "true nature"); it is their parents
who then make them a Jew or a Christian. But if a child's parents were
Muslim, the child would remain a Muslim.[7] According to this teaching,
President Obama was born a Muslim. However, his parents had no role in
directing him away from, or toward, one religion or another. Obama had
written that he "was not raised in a religious household," and his mother
had engaged him in "religious samplings" that "required no sustained
commitment on my part." He noted that in his house "the Bible, the
Koran, and the Bhagavad Gita sat on the shelf alongside books of Greek

---

[5]   Obama, *The Audacity of Hope,* p. 204.

[6]   *Reliance of the Traveller*, see fl.3, o1.0, o1.2 (3), and o8.0 – o8.4.   This
understanding about the penalty for apostasy was based on the teachings of
Muhammad, who said that the penalty for leaving Islam was death – for example
see the following hadiths (*ahadith*) collected by Muhammad ibn Ismail al-
Bukhari: Volume 4, Book 52, Number 260; Volume 9, Book 83, Number 17; and
Volume 9, Book 84, Numbers 57,58, and 64. The hadiths are collections of the
teachings and examples of the prophet Muhammad; those collected by al-Bukhari
are considered the most reliable and authoritative (*sahih*). Those collected by
Abul Husain Muslim bin al-Hajjaj al-Nisapuri are considered the next most
reliable and authoritative, and are also considered *sahih*. A searchable data base
for the Koran and various hadith collections is at the website for the University of
Southern California Center for Muslim-Jewish Engagement:
www.usc.edu/schools/college/crcc/engagement/resources/texts/. The hadiths
mentioned in this handbook can be found at that website.

[7]   Hadith – Muslim, Book 33, Number 6429, and Numbers 6423-6428; and
Hadith - al-Bukhari, Volume 6, Book 60, Number 298.

and Norse and African mythology."[8] Therefore it would appear that according to Muhammad's teachings, Obama grew up as a Muslim by default.

However, in 1988, when he was 26 years old, Obama went to Trinity United Church of Christ in Chicago and heard the Reverend Jeremiah Wright preach a sermon titled "The Audacity of Hope." This sermon talked about a world "where white folks' greed runs a world in need"; Obama was so moved by this sermon that he sat in the pew crying.[9] He wrote that he subsequently

> *was finally able to walk down the aisle of Trinity United*
> *Church of Christ one day and be baptized. It came about*
> *as a choice and not an epiphany...*[10]

Thus, according to the teachings of Muhammad, Obama willingly left Islam as an adult. This would make Obama an apostate facing the death penalty, because according to Sharia Law

> *When a person who has reached puberty and is sane*
> *voluntarily apostatizes from Islam, he deserves to be*
> *killed.*[11]

For Obama to have raised these issues might have required his Muslim audience to make a difficult choice: either sit quietly as an apostate from Islam spoke to them, or walk out during the speech. Obama chose the course that would ensure him a Muslim audience.

On the other hand, this would have been the perfect time for Obama to have talked about the freedom of religion in the United States that allowed Obama Sr. to be there regardless of religious belief, or lack thereof, and allowed Obama Jr. to wait until adulthood before making a choice of

---

[8]   Obama, *The Audacity of Hope*, pp. 202-204.

[9]   Obama, *Dreams from My Father*, pp. 291-295.

[10]   Obama, *The Audacity of Hope*, p. 208.

[11]   *Reliance of the Traveller*, o8.1.

religions, without penalty. Unfortunately, he apparently chose to leave out significant elements of his past in order to accommodate the Muslim belief about apostasy.

However, he did not entirely ignore religious freedom in the United States. Later in his speech he stated

> *Moreover, freedom in America is indivisible from the freedom to practice one's religion. That is why there is a mosque in every state in our union, and over 1,200 mosques within our borders.*

So, for President Obama the freedom of religion in the United States was apparently to be extolled only within the context of it allowing the spread of Islam to "every state in our union."

Morocco recognizing the United States and paying Tribute to the Bey

Further into his speech Obama stated

> *I also know that Islam has always been a part of America's story. The first nation to recognize my country was Morocco. In signing the Treaty of Tripoli in 1796, our second President, John Adams, wrote, "The United States has in itself no character of enmity against the laws, religion or tranquility of Muslims."*

President Obama was either a poor student of history or was ready to alter history for the sake of his Muslim audience. Here is a list of diplomatic treaties our country had with other countries prior to the 1786 Treaty of Peace and Friendship with Morocco:

> Treaty of Amity and Commerce with France (1778)
> Treaty of Alliance with France (1778)
> Treaty of Paris (1783) – Peace Treaty with Great Britain
> Treaty of Amity and Commerce with the King of Prussia (1785)

Obama's mention of the 1796 Treaty of Tripoli was curious. Upon hearing his statement about the recognition of the United States by Morocco, followed by the mention of the Treaty of Tripoli, one could have had the impression that the treaty between the United States and Morocco was called the Treaty of Tripoli (after all, the peace treaty between the United States and Great Britain was called the Treaty of Paris). However, the 1796 Treaty of Tripoli was actually a separate treaty between a young, somewhat weak United States and the Muslim Bey of Tripoli, a branch of the Barbary Pirates that was raiding American ships and enslaving American sailors. This Treaty of Tripoli was in reality a treaty in which the young United States agreed to pay tribute to the Bey so that he would quit attacking American ships! Article 10 of this treaty stated

> *The money and presents **demanded** [my emphasis] by the Bey of Tripoli as a full and satisfactory consideration on his part and on the part of his subjects for this treaty of perpetual peace and friendship are acknowledged to have been recieved [sic] by him...*[12]

Among the American tribute the Bey had received was forty thousand Spanish dollars, gold and silver watches, and diamond rings. The arrival of the American consul in Tripoli was to bring more tribute payments that included an additional twelve thousand Spanish dollars.

In a matter of two sentences in his speech Obama had managed to appeal to his Muslim audience by not only inaccurately presenting history, but by also reminding them about a treaty of submission between a young, weaker United States and a stronger Muslim ruler.

---

[12]   The actual name of this treaty was the Treaty of Peace and Friendship between the United States of America and the Bey and Subjects of Tripoli of Barbary. It can be found at The Avalon Project – Documents in Law, History and Diplomacy, Yale Law School, at
http://avalon.law.yale.edu/18th_century/bar1796t.asp.

Swearing an oath on the "Holy Koran"?

Later in his speech President Obama talked about how "American Muslims have enriched the United States," and he stated

> ...when the first Muslim American was recently elected to Congress, he took the oath to defend our Constitution using the same Holy Koran that one of our Founding Fathers -- Thomas Jefferson -- kept in his personal library.

President Obama was talking about Minnesota Congressional Representative Keith Ellison. But, as a former member of Congress, Obama should have known that the members of the House are sworn in en-masse on the House floor, and the subsequent photograph of Ellison holding his hand on a Koran was just that: a photograph of Ellison with his hand on a Koran. For this photograph, Ellison could have had his hand on any book, and it would have had the same insignificance in terms of him becoming a Congressional Representative. Even Ellison was aware of this distinction. Prior to the ceremony, he said he would be officially sworn in "the same exact way as every other Congressperson-elect who was sworn in":

> We will all stand up and in unison lift our hand and swear to uphold that Constitution, and then later, in a private ceremony, of course I'll put my hand on a book that is the basis of my faith, which is Islam...[13]

But President Obama's version was more appealing to his Muslim audience, and it has become a popular "urban legend."

******In order to give further consideration to this part of President Obama's Cairo speech, we must now separate ourselves from Congressman Ellison, for there is nothing to indicate that anything in the following section pertains to the Congressman's beliefs or to his

---

[13]   John Nichols, "Keith Ellison and the Jefferson Koran," *The Nation - The Beat Blog,* January 3, 2007, accessible at http://www.thenation.com/blog/keith-ellison-and-jefferson-koran.

taking of the Congressional oath, and none such is meant to be implied.******

By talking about the taking of an oath by a Muslim, President Obama steers us in the direction of Islamic considerations about oath taking. For example, according to Sharia Law

> *An oath is only validly effected* [sic] *if sworn by a name of Allah Most High, or an attribute of his entity.*[14]

But even though being sworn in the name of Allah, an oath is not necessarily automatically binding. Muhammad said

> *...and by Allah, Allah willing, if ever I take an oath to do something, and later on I find that it is more beneficial to do something different, I will do the thing which is better, and give expiation for my oath.*[15]

Would breaking one's oath be worth enduring the required expiation? According to Sharia Law and the Koran, the expiation for a broken oath consists of doing one of the following:

1. Free a sound Muslim slave;
2. Feed ten people who are short of money;
3. Provide clothing of any kind for ten such persons, even if it consists of a wraparound or clothing previously washed, though not if ragged;
4. And if one is unable to do any of the above, one must fast for three days.[16]

---

[14]   *Reliance of the Traveller*, o18.3.

[15]   Hadith – al-Bukhari, Volume 4, Book 53, Number 361; also see Volume 5, Book 59, Number 668; Volume 7, Book 67, Number 427; Volume 8, Book 78, Numbers 619-620, 644, and 671; Volume 8, Book 79, Numbers 709-710, 712, and 715; Volume 9, Book 89, Numbers 260-261; and Volume 9, Book 93, Number 644. Also see Hadith - Muslim, Book 15, Numbers 4046, 4050, 4052-4058, 4060, and 4062.

[16]   *Reliance of the Traveller*, o20.2, and Chapter 5, Verse 89 of the Koran.

This attitude about the conditionality of an oath was carried over into Muslim warfare. When Muhammad would appoint a commander to lead a military expedition against unbelievers, he would say to the commander

> *When you lay siege to a fort and the besieged appeal to*
> *you for protection in the name of Allah and His Prophet,*
> *do not accord to them the guarantee of Allah and His*
> *Prophet, but accord to them your own guarantee and the*
> *guarantee of your companions for it is a lesser sin that the*
> *security given by you or your companions be disregarded*
> *than that the security granted in the name of Allah and*
> *His Prophet be violated.*[17]

Muhammad also said

> *An oath is to be interpreted according to the intention of*
> *the one who takes it.*[18]

Does it matter what Muhammad said over a thousand years ago? Yes, because according to the Koran, Muhammad is considered to be the timeless example for how Muslims should conduct themselves.[19]

---

[17]   Hadith – Muslim, Book 19, Number 4294.

[18]   Hadith – Muslim, Book 15, Number 4065. Also see Chapter 2, Verse 225 of the Koran.

[19]   *Verily in the messenger of Allah ye have a good example for him who looketh unto Allah and the Last Day, and remembereth Allah much* (Chapter 33, Verse 21). From *The Meaning of The Glorious Koran*, trans. Marmaduke Pickthall, (1930; rpt. New York: Alfred A. Knopf, 1992). Pickthall was an Englishman who had converted to Islam and was working for the Nizam, the Muslim ruler of Hyderabad, in India. As William Montgomery Watt pointed out in the introduction to this translation (p. xxii)

> *[Pickthall] was given two years' leave from his work by the*
> *Nizam in order to produce the translation, and he was also able*
> *to spend some time in Egypt consulting authorities there. Since*
> *one of these authorities was the Sheykh al-Azhar of the time, the*
> *head of the traditional Islamic university and presumably also*
> *Grand Mufti of Egypt, Pickthall might be said to have something*

And the theoretical idea of swearing on the Koran to uphold the United States Constitution raises an interesting question: is Islam compatible with a representative form of government? According to Ayman al-Zawahiri, the second-in-command of the terrorist group Al-Qaeda, the answer is an emphatic "No." He wrote

> *Know that democracy, that is, "rule of the people," is a new religion that deifies the masses by giving them the right to legislate without being shackled down to any other authority...In other words, democracy is a man-made infidel religion, devised to give the right to legislate to the masses – as opposed to Islam, where all legislative rights belong to Allah Most High: He has no partners. In democracies, however, those legislators [elected] from the masses become partners worshipped in place of Allah. Whoever obeys their laws [ultimately] worships them.*[20]

---

like official approval. Above all, his translation shows how the Koran was understood by devout Muslims about 1930, and still is today.

Pickthall pointed out that his translation had been

> *scrutinised [sic] word by word and thoroughly revised in Egypt with the help of one whose mother-tongue is Arabic, who has studied the Koran and who knows English; and when difficulties were encountered the translator had recourse to perhaps the greatest living authority on the subject.*

Pickthall also wrote that "The Book is here rendered almost literally and every effort has been made to choose befitting language" (p. xxvii). Many of these translated verses have words in brackets; Pickthall wrote that he had inserted these in order to explain the meaning of the verse (p. 20). Muslims consider the Koran to be the infallible Word of Allah "revealed" to Muhammad. Consequently, Pickthall, as a Muslim, had an added incentive in making sure his translation was scrutinized and used "befitting language," because according to Sharia Law, it is apostasy to revile Allah or Muhammad, or to deny any verse of the Koran or to add a verse that does not belong to it – see *Reliance of the Traveller*, o8.7 (4) and (7). Subsequent verses quoted from the Koran are from Pickthall's translation.

[20]   *The Al Qaeda Reader*, edited and translated by Raymond Ibrahim, (New York: Broadway Books, 2007), page 130.

Al-Zawahiri said that blasphemy was "inherent to democracies." He pointed out that not only was the right to make law given to someone other than Allah, but "the power of the nation" superseded the power of Allah. He said that "the principle of equality regarding rights and duties among the citizens of democracies" made for a number of blasphemous situations, including:

1. There was no limit to apostasy "since the Constitution declares freedom of religion."

2. Offensive jihad against infidelity and blasphemy was abolished due to that freedom of religion.

3. Man's dominion over woman was abolished because "in a democracy, women have the right to emulate the dignity and legal status of men."[21]

Al-Zawahiri concluded

> *So anyone who calls for Islam while presenting [a system of] infidelity, such as democracy or socialism, is an apostate infidel...Thus whoever claims to be a "democratic-Muslim" or a Muslim who calls for democracy, is like one who says about himself "I am a Jewish Muslim" or "I am a Christian Muslim" – the one worse than the other. He is an apostate infidel.*[22]

And Sharia Law appears to support Al-Zawahiri's claim that "all legislative rights belong to Allah":

> *There is no disagreement among the scholars of the Muslims that the source of legal rulings for all the acts of those who are morally responsible is Allah Most Glorious.*[23]

---

[21]   Ibid., pp. 133-135.

[22]   Ibid., p. 136.

[23]   *Reliance of the Traveller*, a1.1.

One cannot say for certain how much support among Muslims in general there is for this attitude toward representative forms of government. However, as will be shown below, there is a certain level of support for Al-Qaeda among Muslim Americans. And a 2007 survey of Muslim public opinion in Morocco, Egypt, Pakistan, and Indonesia, showed that 38% shared some or all of Al-Qaeda's attitudes toward the United States.[24]

Some Facts about Muslim Americans

Obama noted how much had been made "of the fact that an African American with the name Barack Hussein Obama could be elected President." And he said that his personal story was not so unique.

> *The dream of opportunity for all people has not come true for everyone in America, but its promise exists for all who come to our shores -- and that includes nearly 7 million American Muslims in our country today who, by the way, enjoy incomes and educational levels that are higher than the American average.*

However, a little over two weeks later, in an interview with a Pakistani journalist, Obama said there were only 5 million Muslims in the United States.[25] Could we have somehow lost 2 million Muslim Americans in the space of two weeks, or was Obama just throwing out numbers?

An apparently more reliable, but less impressive number comes from the 2009 Pew Research Center study about global Muslim populations; this study found that there were only about 2.45 million Muslim Americans in

---

[24]   *Muslim Public Opinion on US Policy, Attacks on Civilians and al Qaeda,* Worldpublicopinion.org, The Program on International Policy Attitudes at the University of Maryland, April 24, 2007, p. 13. Accessible at http://www.worldpublicopinion.org/pipa/pdf/apr07/START_Apr07_rpt.pdf.

[25]   Anwar Iqbal, "Beat extremists you can, says Obama," *Dawn.com, World,* June 21, 2009. Accessible at http://www.dawn.com/wps/wcm/connect/dawn-content-library/dawn/news/world/12-beat-extremists-you-can-says-obama--bi-04.

the United States in 2009.[26] And the claim of nearly 7 million Muslim Americans? This claim was addressed by a 2007 Pew Research Center study titled *Muslim Americans, Middle Class and Mostly Mainstream*. The study noted

> *An ambitious 2001 survey led by researchers from Hartford Institute for Religious Research provided a basis for the frequently cited estimate of 6-7 million Muslim adults and children. The study, sponsored by the Council on American-Islamic Relations [CAIR], attempted to identify every mosque in the U.S. Leaders from a representative sample of mosques were then questioned about a host of issues, including the number of worshippers associated with each one. This study concluded that 2 million Muslims in the U.S. are involved with a mosque, at least tangentially. Based on this number, the authors surmise that "estimates of a total Muslim population of 6-7 million in America seem reasonable." Some critics speculated that mosque representatives may have inflated or otherwise misreported the number of people associated with the mosque, a tendency researchers have found among religious leaders in other faiths.[27]*

And what about Obama's statement that Muslim Americans were above average in terms of education and income? Consider the following data about education from the 2007 Pew Research Center study:[28]

---

[26]   *Mapping the Global Muslim Population* , Pew Research Center, October 2009, p. 25. Accessible at
http://pewforum.org/uploadedfiles/Topics/Demographics/Muslimpopulation.pdf.

[27]   *Muslim Americans, Middle Class and Mostly Mainstream*, Pew Research Center, May 22, 2007, p. 13. Accessible at
http://pewresearch.org/assets/pdf/muslim-americans.pdf.

[28]   Ibid., p. 18.

Education (%)	US Muslims	US General Public
Graduate study	10	9
College grad	14	16
Some college	23	29
HS graduate	32	30
Not HS grad	21	16

In terms of not completing high school or of having only a high school diploma, Muslim Americans had a higher percentage rate than did the general public in the United States. In terms of continuing on for a college education, the general public had a much higher percentage in terms of college attendance and graduation than did Muslim Americans. With regard to graduate studies, the percentage rate for Muslim Americans was barely higher than for the general public. These are not Muslim American educational levels that are "higher than the American average." And it is unlikely that there were any significant changes in these categories between 2007 and 2009.

The 2007 Pew study also looked at household income and home ownership:[29]

Household income	US Muslims	US General Public
$100,000+	16	17
$75-$99,999	10	11
$50-$74,999	15	16
$30-$49,999	24	23
Less than $30,000	35	33
Home owner (%)	41	68

In terms of income, there was a higher percentage of Muslim Americans earning less than $30,000 than for the general public. And the percentage of Muslim Americans who earned in the $30-$49,999 range was slightly higher than that for the general public. However, in the income ranges from $50,000 up, the percentages for the general public were all slightly higher. And in terms of home ownership, the general public had a vastly

---

[29]   Ibid.

15

higher percentage rate of ownership than that of Muslim Americans. Considering that it is unlikely there were any significant changes between 2007 and 2009, this data does not support Obama's claim that Muslim American income levels are "higher than the American average."

"Islam is a part of America": Assimilation, Suicide Bombing, and Al Qaeda

As his speech continued, Obama stated, "So let there be no doubt: Islam is a part of America."

Unfortunately, the 2007 Pew Research Center study raised serious questions about this claim. According to this study, only 43% of Pew's then estimated 2.35 million Muslim Americans thought that Muslims coming to America should adopt American customs. 26% (611,000) of Muslim Americans actually thought that newly arriving Muslims should try to remain distinct from American society, and 15% (352,500) of Muslim Americans did not know or responded "Neither." [30] These last two groups mean there were almost one million Muslim Americans who did not support the idea of newly arriving Muslims becoming a part of American society.

Obama continued by talking about how in the United States we share common aspirations, such as living in peace and security. Here again, the 2007 Pew Research Center study raises questions about these common aspirations. Consider the following:

1. 188,000 Muslim Americans thought that suicide bombings in defense of Islam and <u>against civilian targets</u> could be often or sometimes justified; 117,500 thought that such bombings could be rarely justified. That is a total of 305,500 Muslim Americans who would not rule out such bombings. And the majority of these Muslim Americans were under the age of 30. Of additional concern, 211,500

---

[30]   Ibid., pp. 32-33.

Muslim Americans did not know or refused to say.[31] This means there were over one-half million Muslim Americans who would not categorically rule out suicide bombings in defense of Islam against civilian targets!

2. In 1998 Al-Qaeda declared war on the United States and on September 11, 2001 killed thousands on American soil. In 2004 Osama bin Laden admitted that he had come up with the idea for the September 11th attack. In spite of this, in 2007, 117,500 Muslim Americans still had a favorable view of Al-Qaeda, and 634,500 did not know or refused to say.[32]

3. In spite of the extensive media coverage, only 40% of Muslim Americans believed that Arabs carried out the attacks on September 11th. 28% (658,000) of Muslim Americans said Arabs did not carry out those attacks, and 32% (752,000) did not know or refused to say.[33]

How much is Islam really a part of America, and how many common aspirations are truly shared?

Violent extremism "irreconcilable" with Islam?

President Obama then turned to specific issues, and he talked about the necessity of a partnership in confronting "violent extremism in all of its forms." Such extremism, he pointed out, was

> ...irreconcilable with the rights of human beings, the progress of nations, and with Islam. The Holy Koran teaches that whoever kills an innocent is as -- it is as if he

---

[31] Ibid., pp. 53-54.

[32] Ibid., pp. 54-55.

[33] Ibid., pp.51-52.

*has killed all mankind. And the Holy Koran also says
whoever saves a person, it is as if he has saved all
mankind.*

This paraphrase of Chapter 5, Verse 32 in the Koran, resulting in two rounds of applause from Obama's Muslim audience, was apparently made to support his claim that violent extremism was "irreconcilable" with Islam. However, Obama conveniently stopped before he came to the two verses immediately following (Verses 33-34):

*The only reward of those who make war upon Allah and
His messenger and strive after corruption in the land will
be that they will be killed or crucified, or have their hands
and feet on alternate sides cut off, or will be expelled out
of the land. Such will be their degradation in the world,
and in the Hereafter theirs will be an awful doom; Save
those who repent before ye overpower them. For know
that Allah is Forgiving, Merciful.*

Those "who make war upon Allah and His messenger" are the unbelievers who resist the spread of Islam, and those who "repent" before being overpowered are those who accept Islam before being conquered.

Here are some additional Koranic verses to consider:

Chapter 2, Verse 216: *Warfare is ordained for you, though
it is hateful unto you; but it may happen that ye hate a
thing which is good for you, and it may happen that ye
love a thing which is bad for you. Allah knoweth, ye know
not.*

Chapter 8, Verses 12-13: *When thy Lord inspired the
angels, (saying): I am with you. So make those who
believe stand firm. I will throw fear into the hearts of
those who disbelieve. Then smite the necks and smite of
them each finger. That is because they opposed Allah and
His messenger. Whoso opposeth Allah and His
messenger, (for him) lo! Allah is severe in punishment.*

18

Chapter 8, Verse 39: *And fight them* [disbelievers] *until persecution is no more, and religion is all for Allah. But if they cease, then lo! Allah is Seer of what they do.*

Chapter 8, Verse 67: *It is not for any Prophet to have captives until he hath made slaughter in the land. Ye desire the lure of this world and Allah desireth (for you) the Hereafter, and Allah is Mighty, Wise.*

Chapter 9, Verse 5 (The Verse of the Sword): *Then, when the sacred months have passed, slay the idolaters wherever ye find them, and take them (captive), and besiege them, and prepare for them each ambush. But if they repent and establish worship and pay the poor-due, then leave their way free. Lo! Allah is Forgiving, Merciful.*

Chapter 9, Verse 29: *Fight against such of those who have been given the Scripture as believe not in Allah nor the Last Day, and forbid not that which Allah hath forbidden by His messenger, and follow not the religion of truth, until they pay the tribute readily, being brought low.*

Chapter 9, Verse 123: *O ye who believe! Fight those of the disbelievers who are near to you, and let them find harshness in you, and know that Allah is with those who keep their duty (unto Him).*

Not repenting before being conquered by a Muslim adversary can have dire consequences, as the 600-900 captured males of the Jewish B. Qurayza tribe discovered around 627 AD in Medina as the prophet Muhammad "sent for them and struck off their heads...as they were brought out to him in batches...This went on until the apostle [Muhammad] made an end of them."[34] And then Muhammad "divided"

---

[34]   Muhammad Ibn Ishaq, *The Life of Muhammad (Sirat Rasul Allah)*, trans. Alfred Guillaume, (Karachi: Oxford University Press, 2007), page 464. This book was printed by Mas Printers in Karachi, Pakistan, an Islamic country.

their wives, children, and property among the Muslims.[35] And later, when Kinana b. al-Rabi of the Jewish B. al-Nadir tribe would not reveal where his conquered tribe's treasures were hidden, Muhammad ordered one of his soldiers, "Torture him until you extract what he has," so a fire was built on Kinana's chest.[36]

And Muhammad's violence toward these two tribes was no exception. He ordered the killing of a number of poets simply because they had mocked him with their poetry.[37] After the battle of Badr, he ordered the captive Uqba b. Abu Mu'ayt to be killed. Uqba said, "But who will look after my children, O Muhammad?" Muhammad replied, "Hell," and Uqba was killed.[38] After the Muslims marched triumphantly back into Mecca, Muhammad settled a number of old scores by ordering the killing of some of those who had earlier satirized or insulted him.[39]

In another example, the following *sahih* hadith shows Muhammad's violent approach to killing some apostate criminals:

> *Narrated Anas bin Malik: A group of people from 'Ukl*
> *(or 'Uraina) tribe ----but I think he said that they were*
> *from 'Ukl came to Medina and (they became ill, so) the*
> *Prophet ordered them to go to the herd of (Milch) she-*
> *camels and told them to go out and drink the camels' urine*
> *and milk (as a medicine). So they went and drank it, and*
> *when they became healthy, they killed the shepherd and*
> *drove away the camels. This news reached the Prophet*
> *early in the morning, so he sent (some) men in their*

[35]   Ibid., page 466.

[36]   Ibid., page 515.

[37]   Ibid., pp. 364-369, and pp. 675-676. Also see Hadith – al-Bukhari, Volume 3, Book 45, Number 687, and Volume 4, Book 52, Numbers 270-271; also Hadith - Muslim, Book 019, Number 4436.

[38]   Ibn Ishaq., page 308.

[39]   Ibid., page 551.

pursuit and they were captured and brought to the Prophet before midday. He ordered to cut off their hands and legs and their eyes to be branded with heated iron pieces and they were thrown at Al-Harra [a place of stony ground]*, and when they asked for water to drink, they were not given water. (Abu Qilaba said, "Those were the people who committed theft and murder and reverted to disbelief after being believers (Muslims)* [sic]*, and fought against Allah and His Apostle").* [40]

At one point Muhammad said, "Kill any Jew that falls into your power"; and one of his Muslim warriors, Muhayyisa b. Masud, "leapt upon Ibn Sunayna, a Jewish merchant with whom they had social and business relations, and killed him." When Muhayyisa was berated for doing this by his older brother Huwayyisa, a non-Muslim, Muhayyisa replied that he would have cut off Huwayyisa's head if Muhammad had so ordered it. Huwayyisa exclaimed, "By God, a religion which can bring you to this is marvellous [sic]!" Huwayyisa then became a Muslim. [41] What an interesting incentive for conversion.

It was Muhammad himself who said that he had been commanded to fight until all people became Muslims. [42] And Muhammad also said

I have been favored above the prophets in six things: I have been endowed with consummate succinctness of

---

[40] Hadith – al-Bukhari, Volume 8, Book 82, Number 797. Also see Hadith - al-Bukhari, Volume 1, Book 4, Number 234; Volume 2, Book 24, Number 577; Volume 5, Book 59, Number 505; Volume 7, Book 71, Number 623, and Hadith - Muslim, Book 16, Numbers 4130-4132.

[41] Ibn Ishaq, p. 369.

[42] *Narrated Ibn 'Umar: Allah's Apostle said: "I have been ordered (by Allah) to fight against the people until they testify that none has the right to be worshipped but Allah and that Muhammad is Allah's Apostle, and offer the prayers perfectly and give the obligatory charity, so if they perform that, then they save their lives and property from me except for Islamic laws and then their reckoning (accounts) will be done by Allah"* (Hadith - al-Bukhari, Volume 1, Book 2, Number 24). Also see Hadith – Muslim, Book 1, Number 33.

21

*speech, **made triumphant through dread, war booty has been made lawful for me** [my emphasis]...* [43]

And Muhammad talked about the honor of fighting for the sake of Allah and dying a martyr's death, but forsaking paradise in order to be repeatedly brought back to life and returned to earth to fight and die as a martyr for the sake of Allah. [44]

No links between violent extremism and Islam? Remember, the Koran is the infallible word of Allah, and according to the Koran, Muhammad is not only considered to be the timeless example for how Muslims should conduct themselves, but Muhammad also speaks for Allah. [45] And, according to Sharia Law, it is apostasy to revile Allah or Muhammad, or to deny any verse of the Koran or to add a verse that does not belong to it. [46]

The Rights of Women

President Obama then turned to women's rights. He said

Now, let me be clear: Issues of women's equality are by no means simply an issue for Islam. In Turkey, Pakistan,

---

[43]   *Reliance of the Traveller*, w4.2 (3). Also see Hadith – al-Bukhari, Volume1, Book 7, Number 331, and Volume 1, Book 8, Number 429, where Muhammad stated that war booty had not been lawful for anyone else before him.

[44]   Hadith – Muslim, Book 20, Numbers 4626, 4631, 4634, and 4635. Also, Hadith - al-Bukhari, Volume 1, Book 2, Number 35; Volume 4, Book 52, Numbers 53-54, 72, 216; and Volume 9, Book 90, Numbers 332-333. For an interesting discussion about comparing violence in Judaism, Christianity, and Islam, see Raymond Ibrahim, "Are Judaism and Christianity as Violent as Islam?" *The Middle East Quarterly*, Volume 16, No. 3 (Summer 2009). Accessible at http://meforum.org/2159/are-judaism-and-christianity-as-violent-as-islam.

[45]   *Whoso obeyeth the messenger* [Muhammad] *obeyeth Allah, and whoso turneth away: We have not sent thee as a warder over them* (Chapter 4, Verse 80). Also see Hadith – al-Bukhari, Volume 9, Book 92, Number 385.

[46]   *Reliance of the Traveller*, o8.7 (4) and (7).

Bangladesh, Indonesia, we've seen Muslim-majority countries elect a woman to lead. Meanwhile, the struggle for women's equality continues in many aspects of American life, and in countries around the world.

Obama lauded the fact that certain Muslim countries have had female leaders, while being critical about the status of women's equality in the United States. In reality, "women's equality" is a concept of questionable application under Islam. Consider the following:

1.   The Koran states that if you need witnesses, find two men, or if you cannot find two men, then find one man and two women (Chapter 2, Verse 282). This is also codified in Sharia Law.[47]

2.   Muhammad said, "Isn't the witness of a woman equal to half of that of a man?" The women said, "Yes." He said, "This is because of the deficiency of a woman's mind."[48]

3.   Muhammad went even further in finding deficiencies among women: He said to a group of women, "I have not seen anyone more deficient in intelligence and religion than you. A cautious sensible man could be led astray by some of you." The women asked, "O Allah's Apostle! What is deficient in our intelligence and religion?" He said, "Is not the evidence of two women equal to the witness of one man?" They replied in the affirmative. He said, "This is the deficiency in her intelligence. Isn't it true that a woman can neither pray nor fast during her menses?" The women replied in the affirmative. He said, "This is the deficiency in her religion."[49]

---

[47]   Ibid., o24.7, and o24.10 where, when testimony "concerns things which men do not typically see," if two men cannot be found, then four women can provide testimony.

[48]   Hadith – al-Bukhari, Volume 3, Book 48, Number 826.

[49]   Hadith – al-Bukhari, Volume 1, Book 6, Number 301.

4.   When it comes to inheritance, the Koran states that a
        female will receive only half of that which a male receives
        (Chapter 4, Verse 11). This is also codified in Sharia Law
        and mentioned in hadiths,[50] and it is amply illustrated in
        the Islamic Last Will and Testament available at the web
        site for the Islamic Center of Des Moines, Iowa, under
        "Forms and Services - Other Services"
        (www.goicdm.org).

5.   After defeating the Jewish B. Qurayza tribe, Muhammad
        sold some of that tribe's women "for horses and weapons"
        and took one of the captive women for himself.[51]

6.   Muhammad said that prayers would be annulled if a dog, a
        donkey, or a woman passed in front of the praying people,
        a statement about which Mohammed's young wife Aisha
        complained, but to no avail.[52]

7.   Muhammad said, "Men are already destroyed when they
        obey women."[53]

8.   Muhammad said, "After me I have not left any affliction
        more harmful to men than women."[54]

9.   Muhammad said, "I was shown the Hell-fire and that the
        majority of its dwellers were women who were
        ungrateful." It was asked, "Do they disbelieve in Allah?"

---

[50]   *Reliance of the Traveller*, L6.0. Also see Hadith – al-Bukhari, Volume 4,
Book 51, Number 10; Volume 6, Book 60, Number 102; and Volume 8, Book 80,
Number 731.

[51]   Ibn Ishaq, p. 466.

[52]   Hadith – al-Bukhari, Volume 1, Book 9, Number 490.

[53]   *Reliance of the Traveller*, p28.1 (1).

[54]   Haidth – al-Bukhari, Volume 7, Book 62, Number 33.

(or are they ungrateful to Allah?) He replied, "They are ungrateful to their husbands and are ungrateful for the favors and the good (charitable deeds) done to them. If you have always been good (benevolent) to one of them and then she sees something in you (not of her liking), she will say, 'I have never received any good from you.'"[55]

10.   Muhammad said, "I looked at Paradise and found poor people forming the majority of its inhabitants; and I looked at Hell and saw that the majority of its inhabitants were women."[56]

11.   Muhammad said, "If a husband calls his wife to his bed (i.e. to have sexual relation [sic]) and she refuses and causes him to sleep in anger, the angels will curse her till morning."[57]

12.   Muhammad said, "Lay injunctions on women kindly, for they are prisoners with you having no control of their persons."[58]

13.   According to the Koran, Allah advised husbands that if they feared their wives were being rebellious, the husbands should admonish them, banish them to beds apart, and scourge [whip] them (Chapter 4, Verse 34). Muhammad said "to beat them [wives] but not with severity."[59] This idea is also codified in Sharia Law:

---

[55]   Hadith – al-Bukhari, Volume 1, Book 2, Number 28; and Volume 7, Book 62, Number 125; also Hadith -Muslim, Book 4, Number 1982.

[56]   Hadith – al-Bukhari, Volume 4, Book 54, Number 464; also Volume 7, Book 62, Numbers 124 and 126; and Hadith - Muslim, Book 36, Numbers 6596-6597 and 6600.

[57]   Hadith – al-Bukhari, Volume 4, Book 54, Number 460, and Volume 7, Book 62, Number 122; and Hadith - Muslim, Book 8, Numbers 3366-3368.

[58]   Ibn Ishaq, p. 651.

[59]   Ibid.

a. *If she commits rebelliousness, he keeps from sleeping with her without words, and may hit her, but not in a way that injures her, meaning he may not break bones, wound her, or cause blood to flow. He may hit her whether she is rebellious only once or whether more than once...*[60]

b. *If keeping from her is ineffectual, it is permissible for him to hit her if he believes that hitting her will bring her back to the right path...*[61]

14. "Aisha said that the lady (came), wearing a green veil (and complained to her (Aisha) of her husband and showed her a green spot on her skin caused by beating)...when Allah's Apostle came, Aisha said, 'I have not seen any woman suffering as much as the believing [Muslim] women. Look! Her skin is greener than her clothes!' "[62]

15. Aisha also said, "O womenfolk, if you knew the rights that your husbands have over you, every one of you would wipe the dust from her husband's feet with her face."[63]

16. According to Sharia Law:

a. "Whenever the bride is a virgin, the father or father's father may marry her to someone without her permission, though it is recommended to ask her permission **if she has reached puberty** [my

---

[60] *Reliance of the Traveller*, m10.12.

[61] Ibid., m10.12 (4)(c).

[62] Hadith – al-Bukhari, Volume 7, Book 72, Number 715.

[63] Daniel Ali and Robert Spencer, *Inside Islam: A Guide for Catholics, 100 Questions and Answers*, (West Chester, PA: Ascension Press, 2003), p. 136.

emphasis]. A virgin's silence is considered as permission."[64]

b. "A guardian may not marry his **prepubescent daughter** [my emphasis] to someone for less than the amount typically received as marriage payment by similar brides..."[65]

c. A Muslim man can have up to four wives.[66]

d. Circumcision is obligatory.[67]

e. If the newborn baby is a male, it is recommended that two *shahs* (a one-year old sheep or a two year old goat) be slaughtered. If the newborn baby is a female, it is recommended to slaughter only one *shah*.[68]

f. Unless there is a "pressing necessity," a wife is not allowed to leave the house without her husband's permission, nor may she "permit anyone to enter **her husband's home** [my emphasis] unless he agrees, even their unmarriageable kin. Nor may she be alone with a nonfamily-member male, under any circumstances."[69]

---

[64] *Reliance of the Traveller*, m3.13 (2). With regard to the silence of a virgin equating consent, also see Hadith – Muslim, Book 8, Numbers 3303-3308; and Hadith - al-Bukhari, Volume 7, Book 62, Numbers 67-68; Volume 9, Book 85, Number 79; and Volume 9, Book 86, Numbers 98, and 100-101.

[65] *Reliance of the Traveller*, m8.2.

[66] Ibid., m6.10.

[67] Ibid., e4.3.

[68] Ibid., j15.2.

[69] Ibid., m10.12 (2).

g. Divorce is valid from any husband [no mention of wife] who is sane, has reached puberty, and who voluntarily effects it, although the husband can "commission" his wife to pronounce the divorce by saying "You are divorced."[70]

h. "The indemnity for the death or injury of a woman is one-half the indemnity paid for a man."[71]

17. Muhammad, in his early 50's, married Aisha when she was six years old and consummated their marriage when she was nine years old.[72] Aisha stated that when she went to Muhammad's house as a nine-year-old bride, she took her dolls with her, and her playmates would come to the house to play.[73]

18. A woman came to Muhammad and presented herself to him for marriage. Muhammad said, "I am not in need of women these days." He then married her to another Muslim based on that Muslim's knowledge of the Koran.[74]

And in a glaring example of how Muhammad condoned the rape of female captives from the Mustaliq tribe, we can see that the only problem to be resolved in the *sahih* hadith below was whether or not the ransom the Muslims were expecting for these particular female captives would be affected if the captives were returned pregnant. In response to the question

---

[70] Ibid., n1.1 and n3.3 (3).

[71] Ibid., 04.9.

[72] Hadith – al-Bukhari, Volume 5, Book 58, Numbers 234 and 236; and Volume 7, Book 62, Numbers 64, 65, and 88; also Hadith - Muslim, Book 8, Numbers 3309-3310.

[73] Hadith – Muslim, Book 8, Number 3311, and Book 31, Number 5981; also see Hadith - al-Bukhari, Volume 8, Book 73, Number 151.

[74] Hadith – al-Bukhari, Volume 7, Book 62, Numbers 24, 54, 58, 63, 66, 72 and 79; and Volume 7, Book 72, Number 760; also see Volume 6, Book 61, Numbers 547-548.

about whether the Muslim warriors should therefore engage in coitus interruptus with their rape victims, Muhammad, instead of prohibiting the rapes, merely said that coitus interruptus would not matter because every soul that was destined to be born would be born:

> *Abu Sirma said to Abu Sa'id al Khadri (Allah he pleased with him): 0 Abu Sa'id, did you hear Allah's Messenger (may peace be upon him) mentioning al-'azl* [coitus interruptus]*? He said: Yes, and added: We went out with Allah's Messenger (may peace be upon him) on the expedition to the Bi'l-Mustaliq and took captive some excellent Arab women; and we desired them, for we were suffering from the absence of our wives, (but at the same time) we also desired ransom for them. So we decided to have sexual intercourse with them but by observing 'azl...But we said: We are doing an act whereas Allah's Messenger is amongst us; why not ask him? So we asked Allah's Messenger (may peace be upon him), and he said: It does not matter if you do not do it, for every soul that is to be born up to the Day of Resurrection will be born.*[75]

And Muhammad appeared to have no problem even with the general idea of raping female captives:

> *Narrated Abu Said Al-Khudri: We got female captives in the war booty and we used to do coitus interruptus with them. So we asked Allah's Apostle about it and he said, "Do you really do that?" repeating the question thrice, "There is no soul that is destined to exist but will come into existence, till the Day of Resurrection."*[76]

---

[75]   Hadith – Muslim, Book 8, Number 3371, also Numbers 3372-3376, and Hadith - al-Bukhari, Volume 3, Book 46, Number 718; Volume 5, Book 59, Number 459; and Volume 9, Book 93, Number 506.

[76]   Hadith – al-Bukhari, Volume 7, Book 62, Number 137; also see Volume 3, Book 34, Number 432, and Volume 8, Book 77, Number 600.

The permission to rape female captives appears to be further reinforced in the Koran:

> *And all married women are forbidden unto you save those (captives) whom your right hands possess. It is a decree of Allah for you...* (Chapter 4, Verse 24)

> *O Prophet! Lo! We have made lawful unto thee thy wives unto whom thou hast paid their dowries, and those whom thy right hand possesseth of those whom Allah hath given thee as spoils of war...* (Chapter 33, Verse 50)[77]

With Muhammad considered to be the example for how Muslims should conduct themselves, and Sharia Law making it apostasy to revile

---

[77]   In his CAIR-issued translation of the Koran, Muhammad Asad pointed out in Footnote 58 to Chapter 33, Verse 50 that "one whom his right hand possesses" refers to "a woman taken captive in a 'holy war' (jihad)..." See *The Message of the Qur'an*, trans. Muhammad Asad, (Bristol, England: The Book Foundation, 2003), p. 727. He had earlier noted this equivalency in Footnote 4 on Page 118, and in Footnote 26 on Page 123.

A number of Hadiths reiterate the point that those women "whom your right hands possess" refers to women captured in battle, and also, if those women were already married, that marriage was abrogated by their capture. See Hadith – Muslim, Book 8: The Book of Marriage (Kitab Al-Nikah) - Chapter 29: IT IS PERMISSIBLE TO HAVE SEXUAL INTERCOURSE WITH A CAPTIVE WOMAN AFTER SHE IS PURIFIED (OF MENSES OR DELIVERY) IN CASE SHE HAS A HUSBAND, HER MARRIAGE IS ABROGATED AFTER SHE BECOMES CAPTIVE. Also Hadith – Muslim, Book 8, Numbers 3432-3434.

The abrogation of the previous marriage of a captive woman is actually codified in Sharia Law under a subsection titled "The Rules of Warfare" (*Reliance of the Traveller*, o9.13):

> *When a child or a woman is taken captive, they become slaves by the fact of capture, and the woman's previous marriage is immediately annulled.*

Also see Hadith - al-Bukhari, Volume 7, Book 62, Numbers 2 and 89, and Volume 9, Book 89, Number 321.

Muhammad or deny any verse in the Koran or add a verse to it, it appears that the struggle for women's equality has some major challenges under Islam.

Islam and the Golden Rule

President Obama came to the end of his speech saying

> *There's one rule that lies at the heart of every religion --*
> *that we do unto others as we would have them do unto us.*

This earned applause from his Muslim audience, but unfortunately, there is no concept of the Golden Rule in Islam; non-Muslims are to be treated differently than Muslims. Consider the following:

1. Muhammad said, "I will expel the Jews and Christians from the Arabian Peninsula and will not leave any but Muslim."[78]

2. On his deathbed, Muhammad's last injunction was, "Let not two religions be left in the Arabian peninsula."[79] Consequently, Islam is the only religion allowed in Saudi Arabia.

3. Islamic scholars are in agreement that the "universal message of Islam" has abrogated the "previously revealed religions" and

> *...it is unbelief (kufr) to hold that the remnant cults now bearing the names of formerly valid religions, such as "Christianity" or "Judaism," are acceptable to Allah Most High after He has sent the final Messenger (Allah bless him give him peace) to the entire world.*[80]

---

[78] Hadith – Muslim, Book 19, Numbers 4366-4367.

[79] Ibin Ishaq, p. 689.

[80] *Reliance of the Traveller*, w4.1 (2).

4. According to Sharia Law:

   a. "Retaliation is obligatory" against anyone who intentionally kills another human "without right." However, there are some exceptions where retaliation is not permitted. Among those exceptions are a Muslim killing a non-Muslim.[81]

   b. The indemnity paid for the death or injury of a Jew or Christian is one-third of the indemnity paid for the death or injury of a Muslim.[82]

   c. Zakat (charitable giving) is obligatory for Muslims and one of the five pillars of Islam. However, it "is not permissible to give zakat to a non-Muslim."[83]

   d. A non-Arab man is not a suitable match to marry an Arab woman because Muhammad said, "Allah has chosen the Arabs above others."[84]

   e. In matters pertaining to child custody, if a child is a Muslim, a non-Muslim has no right to the custody of that child.[85]

   f. In matters of inheriting part of an estate, a "Muslim may not inherit from a non-Muslim, and a non-Muslim may not inherit from a Muslim."[86]

---

[81] Ibid., o1.1 and o1.2 (2); also see o1.2 (4) that gives a parent or grandparent the right to kill their child or grandchild with no retaliation allowed.

[82] Ibid., o4.9.

[83] Ibid., h8.24.

[84] Ibid., m4.2 (1)

[85] Ibid., m13.2 (c).

[86] Ibid., L5.2. Also see Hadith - al-Bukhari, Volume 8, Book 80, Number 756, and Hadith – Muslim, Book 11, Number 3928.

g. It is forbidden for a non-Muslim to enter the Sacred Precinct in Mecca "under any circumstances," or to enter any other mosque without permission.[87]

h. Many non-Muslims have historically been allowed to live as subjects in a Muslim state, but with restrictions placed on them (*Al-Dhimma*).[88] These restrictions included:

   1. Having to pay the non-Muslim poll tax (jizya) – this is the "tribute" referred to in Chapter 9, Verse 29 in the Koran.[89]

   2. Dressing differently so as to distinguish themselves from Muslims.[90]

   3. Not being greeted by Muslims with *as-Salamu alaykum* (peace be upon you).

   4. Keeping to the side of the street when travelling.[91]

---

[87]   *Reliance of the Traveller*, o11.7. Also see Chapter 9, Verse 28 of the Koran.

[88]   *Reliance of the Traveller*, o11.0.

[89]   Chapter 9, Verse 29: *Fight against such of those who have been given the Scripture as believe not in Allah nor the Last Day, and forbid not that which Allah hath forbidden by His messenger, and follow not the religion of truth, until they pay the tribute readily, being brought low.*

[90]   Muhammad saw a Muslim wearing two clothes dyed in saffron. He told the Muslim: These are the clothes (usually worn by) the non-believers, so do not wear them (Hadith – Muslim, Book 24, Numbers 5173-5174). According to Sharia Law it is "offensive" to wear the clothes or use the vessels of non-Muslims (*Reliance of the Traveller*, e2.3).

[91]   *Abu Huraira reported Allah's Messenger (may peace be upon him) as saying: Do not greet the Jews and the Christians before they greet you and when you meet any one of them on the roads force him to go to the narrowest part of it.* Hadith – Muslim, Book 26, Number 5389.

5. Not building a structure higher than or as high as the Muslims' buildings.

6. No construction of new churches.

7. No ringing of church bells, display of crosses, recitation of the Torah, or display of funerals or feast days.

i. It is recommended to visit the ill. If the sick person is a non-Muslim subject of the Islamic state (a *dhimmi*), visiting is recommended; if the sick person is a non-Muslim not subject to the Islamic state, visiting is merely permissible.[92]

j. The nature of the consolations offered due to a death depend on who died; "It is recommended to say":

1. To a Muslim who has lost a Muslim relative, "May Allah greaten your reward, perfect your consolation, and forgive your deceased;"

2. To a Muslim who has lost a non-Muslim relative, "May Allah greaten your reward and perfect your consolation;"

3. And to a non-Muslim who has lost a Muslim relative, "May Allah perfect your consolation and forgive your deceased."

For a non-Muslim then, there should be no request for Allah to "greaten" their reward if they are a surviving relative or to forgive them if they are the deceased.[93]

k. When appearing in court, the judge

treats two litigants impartially, seating both in places of equal honor, attending to each, and so

---

[92]   *Reliance of the Traveller*, g1.2.

[93]   Ibid., g6.2.

forth, unless one is a non-Muslim, in which case
he gives the Muslim a better seat.[94]

5. Muhammad said, "No Muslim would die but Allah would admit in
    his stead a Jew or a Christian in Hell-Fire."[95]

6. Muhammad said, "You will fight against the Jews and you will
    kill them until even a stone would say: Come here, Muslim, there
    is a Jew (hiding himself behind me); kill him."[96]

7. A Muslim declared that his Coptic Christian slave would be freed
    after he died. The Muslim subsequently died and the slave was
    freed. However, Muhammad heard about this, revoked the slave's
    freedom, and sold the slave for 800 dirhams.[97]

8. It is unlawful for a non-Muslim man to marry a Muslim woman.[98]

The Koran also distinguishes between Muslims (believers) and non-
Muslims (disbelievers). For example:

> Chapter 4, Verse 89: *They long that ye should disbelieve*
> *even as they disbelieve, that ye may be upon a level (with*
> *them). So choose not friends from them till they forsake*
> *their homes in the way of Allah; if they turn back (to*
> *enmity) then take them and kill them wherever ye find*
> *them, and choose no friend nor helper from among them.*

---

[94]   Ibid., o22.12.

[95]   Hadith – Muslim, Book 37, Numbers 6665-6668.

[96]   Hadith – Muslim, Book 41, Numbers 6981-6985; also see Hadith - al-
Bukhari, Volume 4, Book 56, Number 791.

[97]   Hadith - Muslim, Book 15, Numbers 4115-4118. Also see Hadith – al-
Bukhari, Volume 3, Book 41, Number 598.

[98]   See Hadith – al-Bukhari, Volume 3, Book 50, Number 874; also see
Chapter 2, Verse 221, and Chapter 60, Verse 10 of the Koran, and *Reliance of the
Traveller*, m6.7 (5).

Chapter 4, Verse 101: *And when ye go forth in the land, it is no sin for you to curtail (your) worship if ye fear that those who disbelieve may attack you. In truth, the disbelievers are an open enemy to you.*

Chapter 4, Verse 144: *O ye who believe! Choose not disbelievers for (your) friends in place of believers. Would ye give Allah a clear warrant against you?*

Chapter 5, Verse 51: *Oh ye who believe! Take not the Jews and the Christians for friends. They are friends one to another. He among you who taketh them for friends is (one) of them. Lo! Allah guideth not wrongdoing folk.*

Chapter 5, Verse 55: *Your friend can be only Allah; and His messenger and those who believe, who establish worship and pay the poor-due, and bow down (in prayer).*

Chapter 48, Verses 28-29: *He it is Who hath sent His messenger with the guidance and the religion of truth, that He may cause it to prevail over all religion. And Allah sufficeth as a witness. Muhammad is the messenger of Allah. And those with him are hard against the disbelievers and merciful among themselves...*

There might be "one rule that lies at the heart of every religion," but in this case it is not the Golden Rule.

Conclusion

On June 4, 2009, President Barack Obama stood in Cairo University in Egypt and said

> *So I have known Islam on three continents before coming to the region where it was first revealed. That experience guides my conviction that partnership between America and Islam **must be based on what Islam is, not what it isn't.** [my emphasis]*

36

As we can now see, President Obama's presentation of Islam was unfortunately based heavily on what Islam "isn't." The Islamic sources show that the reality of Islam is starkly different from that presented by Obama. Nevertheless, over a year after this error-laden speech, Obama has now been called our "Educator-in-Chief on Islam."

Was this vast gulf between the reality of Islam and the claims made in a presidential speech intentional, or was it rather the product of a seemingly willful lack of knowledge about Islam? One would think that in preparing a presidential speech, especially a speech of this nature, the subject matter would have been studied and every effort made to be accurate in the presentation. And in this speech the President himself made much of his own knowledge of Islam. Unfortunately, the reasons for this vast gulf between the reality and the claims will remain with the President and his speech writers.

However, if we are to achieve Obama's desired partnership between the United States and Islam, we must start by learning about and acknowledging the reality of Islam, even if much of that reality is incompatible with our Constitutional guarantees of equal rights and freedom of speech and religion. Only by dealing with the reality of Islam can we determine what the true nature of that relationship would be.

And in spite of the rounds of applause from the Muslim audience in Cairo, the Taliban in Afghanistan did not find Obama's speech appealing. One week after this speech, the Taliban issued an official statement saying that "there was nothing in the speech which could reduce and eliminate the extreme hatred and lessen the gaps between the Muslims and the U.S.," and the speech was "another unworkable attempt at misleading Muslims." The Taliban ended their statement by calling for a continuation of the fight against the "unbelievers."[99]

---

[99]   *Declaration by Taliban in Afghanistan on Obama's Address to Islamic Nations*, The Middle East Media Research Institute (MEMRI) Special Dispatch No. 2431, July 5, 2009. Accessible at http://www.memri.org/report/en/0/0/0/0/0/0/3392.htm.

A New Mission for the National Aeronautics and Space Administration (NASA): Helping Muslims Feel Good

I am here in the region, its sort of the first anniversary of President Barack Obama's visit to Cairo and his speech there when he gave what has now become known as Obama's Cairo Initiative where he announced that he really wanted this to be a new beginning of the relationship between the United States and the Muslim world. When I became the NASA Administrator, or before I became the NASA Administrator, he charged me with three things: One was he wanted me to help re-inspire children to want to get into science and math, he wanted me to expand our international relationships, and third, **and perhaps foremost** [my emphasis], *he wanted me to find a way to reach out to the Muslim world and engage much more with dominantly Muslim nations to help them feel good about their historic contribution to science, math, and engineering.*

Charles Bolden, NASA Administrator, during an interview with Imran Garda of "Talk to Al Jazeera," in Cairo, Egypt, aired on June 30, 2010.

Accessible at http://buzzroom.nasa.gov/multimedia/videos/351/, and http://english.aljazeera.net/programmes/talktojazeera/2010/07/20107 1122234471970.html.

38

The Shooting at the Little Rock Army Recruiting Station

> *Mr. Bongo is one of three African leaders accused of embezzlement… It is alleged that the volume of real estate owned by Mr. Bongo's family in France could not have been purchased with official salaries alone. In recent weeks this has been followed by the freezing of Mr. Bongo's bank accounts in France following bribery allegations… critics have long argued that Mr. Bongo's stay in power has been as a consequence of a combination of violence and corruption.*
>
> "The Murky World of Omar Bongo," BBC News, May 21, 2009 (http://news.bbc.co.uk/2/hi/africa/8056309.stm)

June 1, 2010 was the one year anniversary of two tragic events. The first event was the shooting of two United States Army privates by a Muslim convert outside the recruiting station in Little Rock, Arkansas; one private was killed and the other was wounded. The second event was the start of the two day silence about this shooting and the nature of the subsequent response from President Barack Hussein Obama, their Commander-in-Chief.

On June 1, 2009, a little after 10:00 AM, Abdulhakim Muhammad, an American citizen and Muslim convert, drove up to the Army recruiting station in Little Rock, Arkansas. There were two Army privates standing outside. Muhammad opened fire and killed Private William Long, 23 years old, and wounded Private Quinton Ezeagwula, 18 years old. After he was captured, Muhammad said that the shooting was done "for the sake of Allah" and was retaliation for American soldiers supposedly desecrating copies of the Koran and killing or raping Muslims.[1] There was no comment from the Obama administration that day.

---

[1]   "Arkansas: Killing of Soldier 'Justified,' Defendant Says," *The New York Times*, June 9, 2009, accessible at http://www.nytimes.com/2009/06/10/us/10brfs-KILLINGOFSOL_BRF.html.

On June 2, 2009, at about noon, President Obama announced his nomination of then-Republican Congressman John McHugh (New York) to become the Secretary of the Army. During his remarks, Obama stated

> *As a nation, we have a sacred trust with all those who wear the uniform: To always take care of them as they take care of us.*[2]

Congressman McHugh then stepped to the microphone and, speaking without notes, stated that the "most important common good" was "the welfare and the interest" of the members of our military and their families.[3] In spite of these tributes to our military personnel, neither Obama nor McHugh said anything about the shooting of Long and Ezeagwula that had occurred just over 24 hours earlier.

There was no comment on these shootings from the Obama administration until June 3rd. However, this comment consisted of just a press release to Arkansas media outlets and to anyone else who happened to ask the White House Press Office for it.[4]

President Obama's silence on the Little Rock shooting was unusual. After all, on May 31, 2009, abortion doctor George Tiller was shot and killed, resulting in a statement from Obama that same evening expressing his shock and outrage.[5] On June 8, 2009, Obama released a statement offering his condolences on the natural death earlier that same day of President El

---

[2]   http://www.whitehouse.gov/the-press-office/remarks-president-nomination-john-mchugh-secretary-army

[3]   Ibid.

[4]   Comments by senior White House correspondent Major Garrett on *Special Report Online* with Bret Baier, June 3, 2009. Also see comments by Bryan Myrick, "White House statement released on Little Rock recruiting center shooting," *Seattle Conservative Examiner*, June 4, 2009 at http://www.examiner.com/x-4295-Seattle-Conservative-Examiner~y2009m6d4-White-House-statement-on-Little-Rock-recruiting-center-shooting-will-not.

[5]   http://www.whitehouse.gov/the-press-office/statement-president-murder-dr-george-tiller

Hadj Omar Bongo Ondimba of the African country of Gabon;[6] Bongo had assumed office in 1967 and converted to Islam in 1973.[7] On June 10, 2009, Stephen Johns, a security guard, was fatally shot at the U.S. Holocaust Memorial Museum; later that same day, Obama released a statement expressing his shock and sadness.[8]

It is interesting to note that Obama's statements about Tiller, Bongo, and Johns were marked "For Immediate Release" and were so released, while his statement about Long and Ezeagwula was delayed for days. And there was also an interesting difference in the content of the statements about the three shooting incidents. With regard to Tiller, Obama spoke of profound differences over abortion, but said that these differences could not "be resolved by heinous acts of violence."[9] In the shooting of Johns, Obama said, "This outrageous act reminds us that we must remain vigilant against anti-Semitism and prejudice in all its forms."[10] Yet in his statement about a shooting that the suspect said had been done "for the sake of Allah," and because of what American soldiers had supposedly done to Muslims and to the Koran, Obama referred to it only as a non-descript "senseless act of violence," with no mention being made of Allah or of Islam:

> *I am deeply saddened by this senseless act of violence against two brave young soldiers who were doing their part to strengthen our armed forces and keep our country safe. I would like to wish Quinton Ezeagwula a speedy*

[6] http://www.whitehouse.gov/the-press-office/statement-president-death-president-bongo-gabon

[7] See Bongo's obituary at http://www.telegraph.co.uk/news/obituaries/politics-obituaries/5478816/Omar-Bongo.html.

[8] http://www.whitehouse.gov/the-press-office/statement-president-obama-holocaust-museum-shooting

[9] http://www.whitehouse.gov/the-press-office/statement-president-murder-dr-george-tiller

[10] http://www.whitehouse.gov/the-press-office/statement-president-obama-holocaust-museum-shooting

41

recovery, and to offer my condolences and prayers to
William Long's family as they mourn the loss of their
son.[11]

Additionally, one can go to the "Statements and Releases" section of the White House web site (http://www.whitehouse.gov/briefing-room/statements-and-releases) and find the statements for Tiller, Bongo, and Johns. But unfortunately there is no listing there for the statement about Long and Ezeagwula.[12]

Why was there a two day delay in the release of Obama's statement about the shooting on June 1st by a Muslim convert, and why did the resulting statement have a generic approach with a limited distribution? It likely had to do with President Obama's travel schedule. On June 3rd Obama was meeting with Saudi King Abdullah in Riyadh, Saudi Arabia; Saudi Arabia is the birthplace of Islam. On June 4th Obama was in Cairo, Egypt giving an error-laden speech that paid homage to Islam and earned repeated rounds of applause from his Muslim audience. The reception in the Middle East might not have been as warm if Obama had just a few days before nationally criticized a Muslim who had attacked American soldiers "for the sake of Allah."

President Obama felt it worthwhile to promptly express his condolences about the murders of an abortion doctor and a security guard, and on the natural death of the allegedly corrupt, Muslim president of a small African country; these statements were also listed on the White House web site. Unfortunately, for the shooting of two young soldiers who served under his command and for whom he said we have a "sacred trust," his condolences were delayed, generic in nature, limited in distribution, and not listed on the White House web site.[13]

---

[11]   "Obama Issues Statement on Little Rock Shooting," KATV Channel 7 News, Little Rock, Arkansas. Accessible at http://www.katv.com/news/stories/0609/628798.html.

[12]   The author looked at the "Statements and Releases" section on June 28, 2010.

[13]   There appeared to have been a similar distancing by Obama shortly after the massacre at Fort Hood. On November 5, 2009, at about 1:30 PM, United

States Army Major Nidal Malik Hasan entered the Soldiers Readiness Processing Center in Fort Hood, Texas. Hasan started yelling *"Allahu Akbar"* and used two handguns to murder 12 soldiers and one civilian, and wound another 30 people. Hasan was subsequently shot and taken into custody by responding law enforcement officers.

Hasan was an American-born Muslim. Inside his apartment investigators found business cards he had made upon which was written "SOA" (Soldier of Allah). For more details about the shooting, and especially Hasan's ties to Islam, see 1) Raymond Ibrahim, "Nidal Hasan and Fort Hood, A Study in Muslim Doctrine," *Middle East Forum*, November 18, 2009, accessible at http://www.meforum.org/2512/nidal-hasan-fort-hood-muslim-doctrine, and 2) Madeleine Gruen, "The Massacre at Fort Hood," *The NEFA Foundation*, February 16, 2010, accessible at http://www.nefafoundation.org/miscellaneous/nefa_forthood.pdf.

On November 6, 2009 Robert A. George, a NBC blogger, aptly described President Obama's response on the day of the shooting

> *The White House was notified immediately and by late afternoon, word went out that the president would speak about the incident prior to a previously scheduled appearance. At about 5 p.m., cable stations went to the president...But instead of a somber chief executive offering reassuring words and expressions of sympathy and compassion, viewers saw a wildly disconnected and inappropriately light president making introductory remarks. At the event, a Tribal Nations Conference...the president thanked various staffers and offered a "shout-out" [to an individual]... Three minutes in, the president spoke about the shooting, in measured and appropriate terms...Anyone at home aware of the major news story of the previous hours had to have been stunned. An incident like this requires a scrapping of the early light banter...*

See "Obama's Frightening Insensitivity Following Shooting," accessible at http://www.nbcchicago.com/news/politics/A-Disconnected-President.html. For the text of Obama's remarks go to http://www.whitehouse.gov/the-press-office/remarks-president-closing-tribal-nations-conference.

The subsequent Department of Defense report on the Fort Hood massacre mirrored President Obama's refusal to mention Islam in relationship to the Little Rock shooting. In January 2010, the Department of Defense issued an 86 page

Yet it was on May 27, 2009, only a few days before the Little Rock shooting, that President Obama said in a speech at Nellis Air Force Base, Nevada

> *... I want to thank all of you, the men and women in uniform, for your service to our country. We're grateful to you...The fact that you serve each and every day to keep us safe is something that every American is grateful for. And so if I don't do anything else as your Commander-in-Chief, I'm going to make sure that we're there for you just as you've been there for us.*[14]

How soon he forgot.

And even though President Obama refused to acknowledge that Islam was the motivating factor in the Little Rock shooting, the issue did not go away. On January 12, 2010, Abdulhakim Muhammad sent a handwritten

---

report about the shooting: *Protecting the Force: Lessons from Fort Hood*, Report of the DoD Independent Review, January 2010, accessible at http://www.defense.gov/pubs/pdfs/DOD-ProtectingTheForce-Web_Security_HR_13jan10.pdf.

Amazingly enough, there was no mention of Hasan's name in the report; he was referred to merely as "a gunman" and "the alleged perpetrator." There was no mention of his having yelled "*Allahu Akbar*," or mention of the word "Muslim" or of the concept of Soldier of Allah. There was also no mention of Islam in the text of the report. The only reference to Islam occurred in the title of an article ("Islamic") listed among a number of articles in Footnote 22 on Page 18. These are curious omissions considering that Secretary of Defense Robert Gates' instructions to the review panel included

> *I ask that you conduct the Review to identify and address possible gaps and/or deficiencies in the DoD's programs, processes, and procedures related to identifying DoD employees who could potentially pose credible threats to themselves or others...you are to assess the execution and adequacy of Army programs, policies, and procedures as applied to the alleged perpetrator.* (Page A-1)

[14]   http://www.whitehouse.gov/the-press-office/remarks-president-nellis-air-force-base-las-vegas-nevada

letter to the judge explaining why he murdered Private Long and wounded Private Ezeagwula:

To Judge Wright Jr.
From Abdulhakim Muhammad

I'm writing this because I wish to plead guilty...This was a Jihadi attack on infidel forces...I plead to capital murder, attempt capital murder, and the other 10 counts without compulsion without deals...I wasn't insane or post traumatic nor was I forced to do this Act. Which I believe and it is justified according to Islamic Laws and the Islamic Religion. Jihad – to fight those who wage war on Islam and Muslims.

Abdulhakim Muhammad, writing to Judge Herbert Wright Jr. about his shooting of Privates Long and Ezeagwula, letter dated January 12, 2010.

Accessible at http://www.nefafoundation.org/miscellaneous/FeaturedDocs/Ar kansas_v_Muhammed_letterAQAP.pdf.

Made in the USA
Lexington, KY
10 September 2010